SMALL GROUP SERIES

Following Jesus

**Encouragement from the Beatitudes
for a Troubled World**

George S. Johnson

Augsburg Fortress, Minneapolis

Contents

INTERSECTIONS
Small Group Series

Following Jesus
Encouragement from the Beatitudes for a Troubled World

Developed in cooperation with the Division for Congregational Ministries

George S. Johnson, series introduction
David W. Anderson and Rich Gordon, editors
The Wells Group, series design
Gay Bumgarner / Index Stock Photography, cover photo

Scripture quotations are from New Revised Standard Version Bible, copyright 1989 Division of Christian
Education of the National Council of the Churches of Christ in the United States of America. Used by permission.

Manufactured in U.S.A.

0 1 2 3 4 5 6 7 8 9

Introduction

Being a Christian today

A question often asked is, "What does it mean to be a Christian in today's world?" It is a different question than "How do I become a Christian," or "Who is a Christian?" The issue centers on being and relationships more than definitions or procedures. This study explores being Christian in today's world — a place of painful tensions between God's created order and Jesus' wisdom and the ways of contemporary life. The main focus will be on discipleship, a life of following Jesus in a broken world.

Beatitudes and the kingdom of God

Each session in *Following Jesus* will help you and your small group focus on living as God's own child in God's own kingdom. The kingdom of God is the most radical concept ever presented to the human race. It was the center and essence of Jesus' life and teaching. The invitation given by Jesus throughout his ministry was to follow him, which meant to participate in the realization of this kingdom of God on earth as in heaven. Jesus himself illustrates the meaning and purpose of the kingdom as both a present reality and future hope. His message and

life called for a reordering of the present unworkable world order. Instead of greed, violence and domination, Jesus' way follows God's order founded on compassion, harmony and community.

The Beatitudes are a list of brief statements that help us get at what Jesus meant when he talked about this kingdom of God. They summarize what following Jesus is about and what discipleship means. Both Matthew and Luke include them in their gospels. In this study, we will concentrate on the Matthew text (5:3-12). His Jewish audience was experiencing transition. The concerns of this community were very similar to ours. The spirituality called for addresses our longing for a life that satisfies.

Story of Moses sheds light on Beatitudes

In addition to the Beatitudes, a study of the narrative around the birth and calling of Moses is included in each session (Exodus 1-3). This will show in story form how the Beatitudes come alive and relate to everyday situations that we face. To recall the story of Moses will encourage us to recall our stories and share these stories with one another. The decisions people of faith encountered then are some of the same decisions we face today.

We all want our lives and our world to work better. We look for more meaningful relationships and want to live out the compassion and wisdom of Jesus. We need encouragement and empowerment for daily living. The Beatitudes and the story of Moses will combine to demonstrate how right attitudes and healthy relationships lead one to experience a happiness, a satisfaction, a wholeness described in the word *blessed*.

The Eighth Beatitude in each beatitude

The last beatitude on persecution (Matthew 5:11-12) will be used in the discussion of each beatitude. As we live out the attitude and choose priorities related to the beatitude discussed, we will face resistance and pain. The element of persecution is present in each beatitude when experienced in a troubled and broken world. Jesus was always honest about the cost of discipleship.

Being is discovered in doing

The full meaning of the attitudes and relationships talked about in the Beatitudes will not be experienced until we are engaged in living them out. As we participate, as we act in obedience, we will find our "being" is transformed. Each session as a number of action suggestions. You are encouraged to take them seriously. You'll notice that some of the discussion questions offer options to spark your imagination. Don't allow them to limit your response.

Once we become aware that God loves us without any strings attached, we want to develop a relationship with Jesus. These sessions are offered to assist you in that quest, realizing that we develop best while living in community. As you share your stories and listen to the stories of one another with a central focus on the story of God, the Holy Spirit will bind you together and give new meaning to what being Christian is about.

SMALL GROUP SERIES

Welcome into the family of those who are part of small groups! Intersections Small Group Series will help you and other members of your group build relationships and discover ways to connect the Christian faith with your everyday life.

This book is prepared for those who want to make a difference in this world, who want to grow in their Christian faith, as well as for those who are beginning to explore the Christian faith. The information in this introduction to the Intersections small group experience can help your group make the most out of your time together.

Biblical encouragement

"Do not be conformed to this world, but be transformed by the renewing of your minds, so that you may discern what is the will of God—what is good and acceptable and perfect" (Romans 12:2).

Small groups provide an atmosphere where the Holy Spirit can transform lives. As you share your life stories and learn together, God's Spirit can work to enlighten and direct you.

Strength is provided to face the pressures to conform to forces and influences that are opposed to what is "good and acceptable and perfect." To "be transformed" is an ongoing experience of God's grace as we take up the cross and follow Jesus. Changed lives happen as we live in community with one another. Small groups encourage such change and growth.

What is a small group?

A number of definitions and descriptions of the small group ministry experience exist throughout the church. Roberta Hestenes, a Presbyterian pastor and author, defines a small group as an intentional face-to-face gathering of three to twelve people who meet regularly with the common purpose of discovering and growing in the possibilities of the abundant life.

Whatever definition you use, the following characteristics are important.

Small—Seven to ten people is ideal so that everyone can be heard and no one's voice is lost. More than 12 members makes genuine caring difficult.

Intentional—Commitment to the group is a high priority.

Personal—Sharing experiences and insights is more important than mastering content.

Conversational—Leaders that facilitate conversation, rather than teach, are the key to encouraging participation.

Friendly—Having a warm, accepting, non-judgmental atmosphere is essential.

Christ-centered—The small group experience is biblically based, related to the real world, and founded on Christ.

Features of Intersections Small Group Series

A small group model

A number of small group ministry models exist. Most models include three types of small groups:

- *Discipleship groups*—where people gather to grow in Christian faith and life;

- *Support and recovery groups*—which focus on special interests, concerns, or needs; and

- *Ministry groups*—which have a task-oriented focus.

Intersections Small Group Series presently offers material for discipleship groups and support and recovery groups.

For discipleship groups, this series offers a variety of courses with Bible study at the center. What makes a discipleship group different from traditional group Bible studies? In discipleship groups, members bring their life experience to the exploration of the biblical material.

For support and recovery groups, Intersections Small Group Series offers topical material to assist group members in dealing with issues related to their common experience, hurt, or interest. An extra section of facilitator helps in the back of the book will assist leaders of support and recovery groups to anticipate and prepare for special circumstances and needs that may arise as group members explore a topic.

Ministry groups can benefit from an environment that includes prayer, biblical reflection, and relationship building, in addition to their task focus.

Four essentials

Prayer, personal sharing, biblical reflection, and a group ministry task are part of each time you gather. These are all important for Christian community to be experienced. Each of the six chapter themes in each book includes:

- Short prayers to open and close your time together.

- Carefully worded questions to make personal sharing safe, non-threatening, and voluntary.

- A biblical base from which to understand and discover the power and grace of God. God's Word is the compass that keeps the group on course.

- A group ministry task to encourage both individuals and the group as a whole to find ways to put faith into action.

Flexibility

Each book contains six chapter themes that may be covered in six sessions or easily extended for groups that meet for a longer period of time. Each chapter theme is organized around two to three main topics with supplemental material to make it easily adaptable to your small group's needs. You need not use all the material. Most themes will work well for 1½- to 2-hour sessions, but a variety of scheduling options is possible.

Bible based

Each of the six chapter themes in the book includes one or more Bible texts printed in its entirety from the New Revised Standard Version of the Bible. This makes it easy for all group members to read and learn from the same text. Participants will be encouraged through questions, with exercises, and by other group members to address biblical texts in the context of their own lives.

User friendly

The material is prepared in such a way that it is easy to follow, practical, and does not require a professional to lead it. Designating one to be the facilitator to guide the group is important, but there is no requirement for this person to be theologically trained or an expert in the course topic. Many times options are given so that no one will feel forced into any set way of responding.

Group goals and process

1. **Creating a group covenant or contract for your time together will be important.** During your first meeting, discuss these important characteristics of all small groups and decide how your group will handle them.

Confidentiality—Agreeing that sensitive issues that are shared remain in the group.

Regular attendance—Agreeing to make meetings a top priority.

Non-judgmental behavior—Agreeing to confess one's own shortcomings, if appropriate, not those of others, and not giving advice unless asked for it.

Prayer and support—Being sensitive to one another, listening, becoming a caring community.

Accountability—Being responsible to each other and open to change.

Items in your covenant should be agreed upon by all members. Add to the group covenant as you go along. Space to record key aspects is included in the back of this book. See page 60.

2. **Everyone is responsible for the success of the group, but do arrange to have one facilitator who can guide the group process each time you meet.**

The facilitator is not a teacher or healer. Teaching, learning, and healing happen from the group experience. The facilitator is more of a shepherd who leads the flock to where they can feed and drink and feel safe.

Remember, an important goal is to experience genuine love and community in a Christ-centered atmosphere. To help make this happen, the facilitator encourages active listening and honest sharing. This person allows the material to facilitate opportunities for self-awareness and interaction with others.

Leadership is shared in a healthy group, but the facilitator is the one designated to set the pace, keep the group focused, and enable the members to support and care for each other.

People need to sense trust and freedom as the group develops; therefore, avoid "shoulds" or "musts" in your group.

3. **Taking on a group ministry task can help members of your group balance personal growth with service to others.**

In your first session, identify ways your group can offer help to others within the congregation or in your surrounding community. Take time at each meeting to do or arrange for that ministry task. Many times it is in the doing that we discover what we believe or how God is working in our lives.

4. Starting or continuing a personal action plan offers a way to address personal needs that you become aware of in your small group experience.

For example, you might want to spend more time in conversation with a friend or spouse. Your action plan might state, "I plan to visit with Terry two times before our next small group meeting."

If you decide to pursue a personal action plan, consider sharing it with your small group. Your group can be helpful in at least three ways: by giving support; helping to define the plan in realistic, measurable ways; and offering a source to whom you can be accountable.

5. Prayer is part of small group fellowship. There is great power in group prayer, but not everyone feels free to offer spontaneous prayer. That's okay.

Learning to pray aloud takes time and practice. If you feel uncomfortable, start with simple and short prayers. And remember to pray for other members between sessions.

Use page 61 in the back of this book to note prayer requests made by group members.

6. Consider using a journal to help reflect on your experiences and insights between meeting times.

Writing about feelings, ideas, and questions can be one way to express yourself; plus it helps you remember what so often gets lost with time.

The "Daily Walk" component includes material that can get your journaling started. This, of course, is up to you and need not be done on any regular schedule. Even doing it once a week can be time well spent.

How to use this book

The material provided for each session is organized around some key components. If you are the facilitator for your small group, be sure to read this section carefully.

The facilitator's role is to establish a hospitable atmosphere and set a tone that encourages participants to share, reflect, and listen to each other. Some important practical things can help make this happen.

- Whenever possible meet in homes. Be sure to provide clear directions about how to get there.

- Use name tags for several sessions.

- Place the chairs in a circle and close enough for everyone to hear and feel connected.

- Be sure everyone has access to a book; preparation will pay off.

Welcoming

Every small group session begins before any material is read or questions answered. It begins with the sense of welcome, the sights, the sounds, the smiles, the greetings. Coffee and refreshments might be a part of the beginning atmosphere. Other groups may wish to put these at the end. Welcome latecomers without making them feel embarrassed. Use name tags even if you think everyone knows all of the other group members.

The atmosphere created as people gather together is important. In fact, the welcoming atmosphere reflects how one follows Jesus in a troubled world. Group members will have come from a variety of settings, some more edifying than others. How people are received into the group at each session can communicate the openness, delight, interest, care, and attention that will be developed throughout the small group experience.

Focus

Each of the six chapter themes in this book has a brief focus statement. Read it aloud. It will give everyone a sense of the direction for each session and provide some boundaries so that people will not feel lost or frustrated trying to cover everything. The focus also connects the theme to the course topic.

Community building

This opening activity is crucial to a relaxed, friendly atmosphere. It will prepare the ground for gradual group development. Two "Community Building" options are provided under each theme. With the facilitator giving his or her response to the questions first, others are free to follow.

One purpose for this section is to allow everyone to participate as he or she responds to non-threatening questions. The activity serves as a check-in time when participants are invited to share how things are going or what is new.

Make this time light and fun; remember, humor is a welcome gift. Use 15 to 20 minutes for this activity in your first few sessions and keep the entire group together.

During your first meeting, encourage group members to write down names and phone numbers (when appropriate) of the other members, so people can keep in touch. Use page 59 for this purpose.

Discovery

This component focuses on exploring the theme for your time together, using material that is read, and questions and exercises that encourage sharing of personal insights and experiences.

Reading material includes a Bible text with supplemental passages and commentary written by the topic writer. Have volunteers read the Bible texts aloud. Read the commentary aloud only when it seems helpful. The main passage to be used is printed so that everyone operates from a common translation and sees the text.

"A Further Look" is included in some places to give you additional study material if time permits. Use it to explore related passages and questions. Be sure to have your own Bible handy.

Questions and exercises related to the theme will invite personal sharing and storytelling. Keep in mind that as you listen to each other's stories, you are inspired to live more fully in the grace and will of God. Such exchanges make Christianity relevant and transformation more likely to happen. Caring relationships are key to clarifying one's beliefs. Sharing personal experiences and insights is what makes the small group spiritually satisfying.

Most people are open to sharing their life stories, especially if they're given permission to do so and they know someone will actively listen. Starting with the facilitator's response usually works best. On some occasions you may want to break the group into units of three or four persons to explore certain questions. When you reconvene, relate your experience to the whole group. The phrase "Explore and Relate," which appears occasionally in the margin, refers to this recommendation. Encourage couples to separate for this smaller group activity. Appoint someone to start the discussion.

Wrap-up

Plan your schedule so that there will be enough time for wrapping up. This time can include work on your group ministry task, review of key discoveries during your time together, identifying personal and prayer concerns, closing prayers, and the Lord's Prayer.

The facilitator can help the group identify and plan its ministry task. Introduce the idea and decide on your group ministry task during "Wrap-up" time in the first session. Tasks need not be grandiose. Activities might include:

- Ministry in your community, such as "adopting" a food shelf, clothes closet, or homeless shelter; sponsoring equipment, food, or clothing drives; or sending members to staff the shelter.

- Ministry to members of the congregation, such as writing notes to those who are ill or bereaved.

- Congregational tasks where volunteers are always needed, such as serving refreshments during the fellowship time after worship, stuffing envelopes for a church mailing, or taking responsibility for altar preparations for one month.

Depending upon the task, you can use part of each meeting time to carry out or plan the task.

In the "Wrap-up," allow time for people to share insights and encouragements and to voice special prayer requests. Just to mention someone who needs prayer is a form of prayer. The "Wrap-up" time may include a brief worship experience with candles, prayers, and singing. You might form a circle and hold hands. Silence can be effective. If you use the Lord's Prayer in your group, select the version that is known in your setting. There is space on page 62 to record the version your group uses. Another closing prayer is also printed on page 62. Before you go, ask members to pray for one another during the week. Remember also any special concerns or prayer requests.

Daily walk

Seven Bible readings and a thought, prayer, and verse for the journey related to the material just discussed are provided for those who want to keep the theme before them between sessions. These brief readings may be used for devotional time. Some group members may want to memorize selected passages. The Bible readings can also be used for supplemental study by the group if needed. Prayer for other group members can also be part of this time of personal reflection.

A word of encouragement

No material is ever complete or perfect for every situation or group. Creativity and imagination will be important gifts for the facilitator to bring to each theme. Keep in mind that it is in community that we are challenged to grow in Jesus Christ. Together we become what we could not become alone. It is God's plan that it be so.

For additional resources and ideas see *Starting Small Groups—and Keeping Them Going* (Minneapolis: Augsburg Fortress, 1995).

1 Awakening the Heart

Focus

To discover anew that our positive response to God's love and Jesus' invitation to follow him brings us into a new experience of what is real, what is important, and what is satisfying.

Community building

For setting small group goals, see page 7.

After giving your name and place of birth, choose one of the following questions. Share your answer with the group in one or two minutes.

- How did your parents meet? What do you know about their courtship?
- Describe something your father or mother considered important. How did you learn this?
- Tell about the friendships you grew up with and favorite games you played.

Take a minute for each group member to share three things that make him or her happy. Little things are okay.

Option

Tell about a time when you needed to get help, or when you could not do it alone.

Opening prayer

Send your Holy Spirit into our midst, that we might experience a new awareness of your love and presence. Open our hearts and minds to listen to one another as we share, as we study, and as we pray together. Amen.

Matthew 5:3

[3] **"Blessed are the poor in spirit, for theirs is the kingdom of heaven."**

The Beatitudes

The Beatitudes are the blessings Jesus extended at the beginning of the Sermon on the Mount (Matthew 5:3-12). They are not always easily understood or made practical for our daily life situations. They are brief statements that describe the Christian experience and challenge us to both grow in our faith commitment and enlarge our capacity for compassion.

One can observe that they are neither commandments to obey nor a summary of what God has done to save us. Rather, they lift up a vision of a new social order where God reigns. Luke's version of the First Beatitude (Luke 6:20) says simply: "Blessed are you who are poor." Neither version is more correct. Neither extols poverty as a virtue. Both Matthew and Luke emphasize that, according to the teaching of Jesus, one is better off if one lives realizing there is a God. The concept of "poor in spirit" refers to an attitude of being open to and dependent on God. It says there is something beyond the material level of reality. It is the experience of being in touch with spiritual realities that energize and transform our lives.

■ When are you most open to the spiritual dimension of life?

Choose one or two and explain.

a. When I am experiencing a crisis or loss.
b. When I take time to connect with nature.
c. When I hear a good sermon or Bible study.
d. Music or art connects me to the spiritual.
e. When I hear the cries of hurting people.
f. In my quiet time or times of solitude.
g. Children help me the most because . . .
h. I don't know that I am very open to a spiritual reality. Maybe it's because . . .
i. When I am part of a worship service.
j. Other.

Assign someone to re-
search various biblical
translations.

■ What does the term *blessed* mean to you? When is the
term used in conversation?

■ Tell the group about a friend or someone you have read
about who experienced a life change that could be attrib-
uted to God's presence in his or her life. You may wish to
tell your own story.

■ Jesus said, "Unless you change and become like children,
you will never enter the kingdom of heaven" (Matthew
18:3). It is said that children are perhaps more open to
faith in God. Why might that be? Can you share an example?

■ In your opinion, what hinders many people from being
"poor in spirit" or open to God's presence and direction?
Remember, there is no one correct answer.

Choose one or two
and explain.

    a. Their upbringing in the home didn't emphasize it.
    b. The pull of materialism or prosperity.
    c. Religion is seen as following rules or beliefs rather
       than healthy relationships.
    d. Easier to conform to the expectations of others.
    e. Needing God's help is seen as weakness.
    f. Inadequate teaching from the church.
    g. Only the material world is real or important.
    h. Other.

■ Think of ways you have been blessed (satisfied) by being
aware of moments of spiritual transformation or amazement. For example, a story told in a sermon or movie,
being changed through prayer, taking time to listen or
help. What has helped to awaken your heart?

A further look

Explore and relate.
Explore in groups of
three or four; then
relate a brief summary
to the entire group.

Read the Song of Mary, the Magnificat, in Luke 1:46-55.

■ How does Mary indicate a life "poor in spirit"?

■ How can these verses affect your thoughts, feelings, and
actions?

Exodus 3:1-8a

Read aloud.

1 Moses was keeping the flock of his father-in-law Jethro, the priest of Midian; he led his flock beyond the wilderness, and came to Horeb, the mountain of God. 2There the angel of the LORD appeared to him in a flame of fire out of a bush; he looked, and the bush was blazing, yet it was not consumed. 3Then Moses said, "I must turn aside and look at this great sight, and see why the bush is not burned up." 4When the LORD saw that he had turned aside to see, God called to him out of the bush, "Moses, Moses!" And he said, "Here I am." 5Then he said, "Come no closer! Remove the sandals from your feet, for the place on which you are standing is holy ground." 6He said further, "I am the God of your father, the God of Abraham, the God of Isaac, and the God of Jacob." And Moses hid his face, for he was afraid to look at God. 7Then the LORD said, "I have observed the misery of my people who are in Egypt; I have heard their cry on account of their taskmasters. Indeed, I know their sufferings, 8and I have come down to deliver them from the Egyptians . . ."

Moses and the burning bush

Moses was a key figure in the drama of God's saving activity as it unfolds in the Scriptures. His encounter with the burning bush was a spiritual experience about what is real, what is important, and what satisfies. It took place during his everyday routine.

Moses left Egypt because he had killed an Egyptian (Exodus 2:11-12). In the process of his personal exodus, it is likely he became distant from his spiritual roots as well. Then Moses encountered God anew in the land of Midian and a new world was opened up to him. It was one of those "aha" moments. Moses experienced what it meant to be "poor in spirit," to be open to and dependent on God. This experience of the awakening of the heart prepared him for a calling to be God's instrument of liberation. Notice the physical and tangible element to this encounter with the living God.

If this study theme is used for more than one small group session, introduce subsequent sessions with a "Community Builder" and "Opening Prayer" and end with "Wrap-up."

Discuss as a group.

- What tangible, visual things are present in worship that help you connect with God and the spiritual dimension of life?

- Moses' experience with the burning bush happened while "keeping the flock." Share with the group a time when you encountered the presence of God as part of your daily routine apart from your church activities.

■ Moses' experience may not be our exact experience, yet there are some elements of his experience that help us see how someone experiences being "poor in spirit." Place a "yes" before those elements you see in the story and a "no" before those you do not see.

___ A call for Moses to repent of his sins.
___ The use of God's Word, the Scriptures.
___ Something hard to explain to his spouse.
___ An openness to mystery and the unexplainable.
___ Doubt and questions.
___ A conversion experience.
___ Music and/or liturgy.
___ A sense of community or group support.
___ God getting through in a dramatic way.
___ Feelings of fear, awe, and amazement.

■ Choose one of the above elements and tell how it has played a part in an experience of God in your life, to what is real and important.

■ God told Moses to remove his sandals because he was standing on holy ground. What do you think was the significance of this?

Choose one and explain.

a. A common religious practice of his day showing humility.
b. "Pay attention, I have something important to say."
c. What you are experiencing is sacred, holy.
d. It may be a pasture but right now it is a house of God.
e. Doing something physical shows that you are ready to stop and really listen.
f. Other.

■ Tell about a time when you needed to "take off your shoes," when you sensed you were standing on holy ground. Are there some worship experiences when you have felt this way? Explain.

■ How does this beatitude and/or story of Moses' experience with the burning bush encourage your faith journey? How does it challenge you?

■ Are confessing our sins and realizing our need for forgiveness part of being "poor in spirit?" Explain.

■ Sing together "Jesus Loves Me."

Consider this

A survey has indicated that 37 percent of the people questioned have had what they call a religious experience. Yet most do not share it with anyone. How have you reacted to others who have shared a religious experience? Why might you not share your experience with others?

A further look
Explore and relate.

Read Matthew 7:24-29. Our spiritual experiences are always meant to encourage us, build healthy relationships, prepare us for life, and call us to new tasks.

■ Where do you need encouragement right now?

Discovery

Matthew 5:10

10 "Blessed are those who are persecuted for righteousness' sake, for theirs is the kingdom of heaven."

Resistance and suffering

In most of the six themes we will deal briefly with this last beatitude, the element of resistance and suffering encountered when we enter more fully into the experiences of the other beatitudes. Whenever Jesus taught or helped people, there was often some form of opposition or criticism. His wisdom was contrary to conventional wisdom and was considered subversive by some. Jesus was always honest about the cost of discipleship and the reality of opposition both from within and from society. The small group movement in Latin America known as Base Christian Communities often approaches a Gospel lesson with three questions: What did Jesus do or say? What does it mean for us? Who would stand to lose in this situation if Jesus' words were carried out?

■ Who would stand to lose if more people would be "poor in spirit" . . . transformed by the power of God in their lives . . . living in humble dependence upon God's love, help, and guidance?

■ How do you handle criticism from others when you are attempting to follow your conscience?

■ How can your small group help you face the challenge of following Jesus?

Community building through our actions

Choose one of these options that you are willing to do before your next session together. Make it a way of entering more fully into this beatitude. Let the group know what your choice is. It's okay to pick more than one.

- Begin a journal. Write down some of the ideas shared in your group, what you learned, how you felt, and questions that came to your mind.

- Find a time to share with a family member or a close friend what you think being "poor in spirit" means and why a person "poor in spirit" is fortunate.

- Be an encourager. Write a thank-you note to someone who has helped you to be more open to the reality and presence of God. Let them know what they did or said that encouraged you.

- Look and listen for examples in the daily news or your work world where you sense people are having a burning bush experience. Come ready to share it.

- Find or create a tangible, visual object that you can place in a strategic location in your living area that will become a concrete (sacramental) reminder of God's saving presence. Bring it to the next session.

- Tell one other person this week that you are in a small group. Answer any questions that person may have about your group experience.

- Commit yourself to memorizing the Beatitudes and begin with Matthew 5:3 this week.

A further look

Explore and relate.

Read Matthew 12:1-14.

- What was in Jesus' teaching that caused such resistance?

- Where do you see it present today?

- How does this resistance influence your understanding of the Christian faith?

Wrap-up

See page 10 in the introduction for a description of "Wrap-up."

Before you go, take time for the following:

- ■ **Group ministry task**

- ■ **Review**

Ongoing prayer requests can be listed on page 61. See page 62 for suggested closing prayers.

- ■ **Personal concerns and prayer concerns**

- ■ **Closing prayers**

Daily walk

Bible readings

Day 1 Luke 18:9-14
Which person was poor in spirit. Why?

Day 2 Matt. 9:10-12
Who are the "well" . . . the "sick"?

Day 3 Luke 19:1-10
What was Zacchaeus' burning bush experience?

Day 4 Matt. 16:24-26
What makes us open to God?

Day 5 Psalm 1:1-3
Who is blessed (happy) and why?

Day 6 Psalm 41:1-3
Who is blessed (happy) and why?

Day 7 Psalm 32:1-2
Who is blessed (happy) and why?

Thought for the journey

"The first beatitude is not a glorification . . . of poverty or hunger. But it is a declaration of the priority of those in need in the policy of God's reign."

From *Augsburg Commentary on the New Testament: Luke* by David L. Tiede, copyright © 1988 Augsburg Publishing House.

Prayer for the journey

Keep us open, Lord, to the many ways you come to us. May our lives be transformed so that we might know what is real, what is important, and what truly satisfies. Amen.

Verse for the journey

"Blessed are the poor in spirit, for theirs is the kingdom of heaven" (Matthew 5:3).

2 Becoming Wounded Healers

Focus

To remember that dark times of grief and pain can be teachable moments and pathways to blessings, and that we can learn from Jesus how to be sensitive to the suffering of others.

Community building

Choose from the following as time permits and as members feel comfortable sharing.

Option

Take three to five minutes to walk through the immediate area of your meeting place, or just outside if weather permits, to observe an object, happening, or symbol that suggests disharmony or pain. Tell the group about it.

■ As you go around the circle giving your name, tell how you got your name and how you feel about it. Do you have, or have you had, any nicknames?

■ Choose one of these three and share your answer with the group:

  a. Tell about a time when your feelings were hurt, when you felt let down, or were treated unfairly. What helped you through it?

  b. Tell about a time you broke up with a boyfriend or girlfriend. What helped you through it?

  c. Tell about a time when you experienced grief or pain over the suffering of someone else (a person or group of people).

■ Have people report activity on their assignments from your last session. Review briefly what is remembered from chapter 1.

Opening prayer

We are grateful, God, for another day to live, to love, and to be loved. Open us to both the pain and joy that come from following Jesus. Amen.

Matthew 5:4

4 "Blessed are those who mourn, for they will be comforted."

Suffering and compassion

Among other things, Jesus is referred to as a "man of sorrow" and "acquainted with grief." His teachings often included a dimension of life that embraced the redemptive power in suffering. While he did not encourage people to pursue pain or glorify sorrow, he did demonstrate and teach that to be compassionate is to enter into the suffering of others. To mourn may not always mean to weep tears, but it does mean to be deeply concerned to the point of action.

"Blessed are you who weep now, for you will laugh," is the parallel verse from Luke 6:21. It is combined with its opposing woe: "Woe to you who are laughing now, for you will mourn and weep" (Luke 6:25). Both Matthew and Luke remind us that we not only mourn our shared brokenness (sin), we also are called to share in the sorrow and agony of those who suffer at the hands of a sinful society or system.

Following Jesus teaches us to embrace the dark moments of life rather than deny them or make excuses for them. Darkness can include any experience of grief or pain that accompanies our relationships. We accept and address darkness when we take time to listen and be present to each other in our struggles. Such an embrace gives birth to newness and blessing.

Discuss as a group.

- Share about a time when you saw one of your parents, another family member, or a close friend grieving. What were the circumstances? How did it affect you?

- What things do you think Jesus was talking about when he said, "Blessed are those who mourn"? What are we to mourn?

Choose one or two and explain.

    a. Our own broken relationships, our sins.

    b. The suffering we experience when we become ill or face a personal crisis.

    c. The suffering we experience when we are unjustly treated.

    d. The suffering of family and friends that causes sorrow in us.

    e. Universal suffering through such things as poverty, religious wars, or natural disasters.

    f. The pain of an addiction.

    g. Other.

■ Which of the above would be the cause of most mourning in our society today? In the church? In you?

Consider this

"When things go well it is possible to live for years on the surface of things; but when sorrow comes, a person is driven to the deeper things of life." —William Barclay

■ Have you ever experienced what Barclay is talking about? Explain.

■ In his book *The Wounded Healer*, Henri Nouwen reminded us that we are not always able to eliminate the pain of others. We are called to share their pain and darkness in such a way that new hope is experienced. How do we do this?

Choose one and share an example of how it was true for you or someone you know.

    a. Not having words to say but just being present.
    b. Willingness to learn about the root causes of the hurt.
    c. Being open to face to face encounters with people struggling for personal survival.
    d. Finding someone who has been where I am, who understands.
    e. Asking the hard questions with compassion.
    f. Being honest enough to recognize limitations, failure, and pain.
    g. Being comfortable with tears.
    h. Other.

■ Jesus became a servant, obedient to God unto death. He was tempted on all points like we are, but without sin. He was misunderstood, rejected, and falsely accused. Jesus was a wounded healer. How does knowing this help us? How did Jesus embrace darkness?

■ In which of the following situations do you think you would be most helpful by entering into the pain of another or sharing in the experience of darkness? Why?

    a. The wound of loneliness.
    b. Some form of addiction.
    c. Having lost touch with God.
    d. Unemployment/career crisis.
    e. Doubts about religion/God/church.
    f. Loss of a loved one.
    g. Terminal illness.
    h. Poverty/hunger.

i. Wound of rejection.
　　j. Childlessness.
　　k. Others.

■ Think of ways that "mourning" has been encouraged where you have worshiped or in your community. Share them with the group.

Consider this

. . . Dorothy was a perpetual member of the third grade church school class. Every child in the church knew that, when you arrived at the third grade in . . . Sunday School, Dorothy would be in your class. She had even been in the class when some . . . parents were in the third grade. Dorothy was in charge of handing out pencils, checking names in the roll book, and taking up the pencils. . . . It was much later . . . that the world told us that Dorothy was someone with Down syndrome. . . . When Dorothy died, in her early fifties — a spectacularly long life for someone with Down syndrome — the whole church turned out for her funeral. No one mentioned that Dorothy was retarded or afflicted. Many testified to how fortunate they had been to know her.

From *Resident Aliens* by Stanley Hauerwas and William H. Willimon. (Nashville: Abingdon Press, 1989), 93.

■ What in this story touches you in a special way?

■ How was Dorothy a wounded healer?

■ Can you think of situations where adversity became an opportunity to witness to God's love and presence?

Remember, if this study theme is used for more than one small group session, introduce subsequent sessions with a "Community Builder" and "Opening Prayer" and end with "Wrap-up."

Discovery

Exodus 1:22—2:4

22 Then Pharaoh commanded all his people, "Every boy that is born to the Hebrews you shall throw into the Nile, but you shall let every girl live."

1 Now a man from the house of Levi went and married a Levite woman. 2 The woman conceived and bore a son;

and when she saw that he was a fine baby, she hid him three months. ³When she could hide him no longer she got a papyrus basket for him, and plastered it with bitumen and pitch; she put the child in it and placed it among the reeds on the bank of the river. ⁴His sister stood at a distance, to see what would happen to him.

Discuss as a group.

■ If you had been an Egyptian when Pharaoh commanded that the Hebrew male babies be thrown in the Nile River, how do you think you would have responded?

    a. I'm glad I'm not Hebrew. Those poor people.
    b. The government must know something I don't know.
    c. I love my country, right or wrong. Love it or leave it.
    d. Let's move away so we don't have to get involved.
    e. When is the next protest rally? I'm going.
    f. I'm going to pray for a change of heart for Pharaoh.
    g. I want to meet Hebrews and share their pain.
    h. Other.

■ If you had been Moses' mother and found yourself pregnant at that time, which of the following reactions would you have had?

    a. Blame God.
    b. Self-pity.
    c. Anger at Pharaoh.
    d. Seeking other's support.
    e. Others are suffering too.
    f. Resigned to fate.
    g. Want to make a basket.
    h. Pray for a miracle.
    i. Weep with despair.
    j. Other.

■ From your own experience, what are some things to avoid in trying to be helpful to people who are going through dark times?

Explore and relate.

■ Where do you see "basket making" (Exodus 2:3) in the community or nation where you live? That is, where are the signs of hopefulness or stories of people taking action rather than complaining or giving up?

Consider this

Leaders (and followers) need to learn not to inflict pain, but to bear pain. . . . If you're bearing pain properly . . . you ought to have the mark of struggle. One ought to have bruised shins and skinned knees.

From *Leadership Jazz* by Max De Pree (New York: Doubleday, 1992), 139.

■ What are some of the marks of struggle you carry? What are some skinned knees you see in a church you are familiar with or a member of?

A further look

Read text aloud and answer as a group.

Read Romans 12:9-15.

■ How do Paul's exhortations help us "Rejoice with those who rejoice, weep with those who weep" (12:15)?

■ Share a time when another person's affection, honor, zeal, patience, prayers, generosity, and/or hospitality made a difference in your life.

Discovery

Matthew 5:10-12

[10] "Blessed are those who are persecuted for righteousness' sake, for theirs is the kingdom of heaven.
  [11] "Blessed are you when people revile you and persecute you and utter all kinds of evil against you falsely on my account. [12] Rejoice and be glad, for your reward is great in heaven, for in the same way they persecuted the prophets who were before you."

Discuss as a group.

In the first chapter of Exodus we learn that a new king came to power in Egypt who did not know Joseph. Joseph's people, the Hebrews, were growing in numbers and influence. The new king instilled a fear that the Hebrews might leave Egypt. It resulted in a form of genocide, the killing of newborn males.

■ Why do you think Pharaoh took such severe action against the Hebrews?

■ Do those same elements invite domination and violence today? Explain.

- Who stood to gain and who stood to lose in the story of fear, violence, and death surrounding Moses' birth and the eventual call for liberation (see Exodus 3:7-8)?

- Watch for signs of mourning in the news you read or hear in the coming week. Where do you feel the nudge to help, the desire to get more involved? Come ready to share your thoughts at the next session.

Explore and relate.

- The Eighth Beatitude reminds us that following Jesus puts us on a collision course with oppressive regimes, institutions, and laws as well as our own greed and tendency toward violence. How have you experienced this opposition? Which side have you been on?

Consider this

Respond to these two quotes in light of your study of "Becoming Wounded Healers."

"I think I have received a new understanding of the meaning of suffering. I came away more convinced than ever before that unearned suffering is redemptive."

—Martin Luther King, Jr., as he emerged from one of his early prison experiences.

"Everything I've ever learned well, I've learned from pain . . . and no pain is more poignant and deafening than the pain that comes in relationships."

From *I Asked for Intimacy* by Renita J. Weems (San Diego: LuraMedia, 1993), 61.

A further look

Read 2 Corinthians 4:7-12.

- How can the experience described by Paul be an encouragement to your own life as a wounded healer?

- When have you felt afflicted but not crushed?

Wrap-up

See page 10 in the introduction for a description of "Wrap-up."

Before you go, take time for the following:

- ■ **Group ministry task**

- ■ **Review**

Ongoing prayer requests can be listed on page 61. See page 62 for suggested closing prayers.

- ■ **Personal concerns and prayer concerns**

- ■ **Closing prayers**

Daily walk

Bible readings

Day 1   Isaiah 61:1-4
Called to comfort all who mourn.

Day 2   Luke 19:41-44
Jesus weeps over Jerusalem.

Day 3   Isaiah 53:1-3
He was a man of sorrow.

Day 4   Psalm 30:4-5
Joy comes in the morning.

Day 5   1 Cor. 12:24b-26
One suffers, all suffer.

Day 6   Jer. 31:15-17
Rachael weeps for her children.

Day 7   John 11:28-37
Jesus weeps at death of Lazarus.

Thought for the journey

To minister to others calls for a recognition of the suffering of one's own heart, which makes our wounds available as a source of healing.

Prayer for the journey

God, help us to enter more fully into our own grief as well as the pain and sorrow of others so that we might experience new hope and courage to go forward through your Son, Jesus Christ. Amen.

Verse for the journey

"Weeping may linger for the night, but joy comes in the morning" (Psalm 30:5).

3 Celebration of Discipline

Focus

A disciple of Jesus is one who learns, who is teachable, and who seeks to follow. Learning requires discipline and humility to open the door to new discoveries and experiences.

Community building

Option

Blow up three or four balloons. Get into circles of four to six people and sit close together. Sit on your hands. Pass the balloon around the circle with your feet, making sure everyone touches it. Then reverse the direction. Try two balloons going in opposite directions. Have fun cooperating.

Think about the helpful things you have done in the last month for which you did not get paid. Tell the group about your experience, the results, and the feelings you had.

■ Take turns sharing with each other something that you learned this past week that you found useful or interesting, or something that surprised you. Or tell the group about something that you learned from a parent, grandparent, or guardian that was helpful.

■ Tell about a time when someone's gentleness (humility) resulted in a positive experience. Or tell about a favorite teacher you had in school. How did that person help you learn?

Opening prayer

Thank you, Lord, for the blessings of this past week, for food and shelter, for friends and family, for work and play, for learning opportunities and experiences that have taught us how to live with compassion toward others. Bless our time together. Amen.

Matthew 5:5

5 "Blessed are the meek, for they will inherit the earth."

The mysterious strength of meekness

The Greek word for "blessed" refers to those who are to be congratulated or who are fortunate or well-off. It describes someone whose situation in life reflects that they are living in right relationship to God, self, and others.

"Blessed" is an enthusiastic and joyful declaration of good fortune that includes both the here and now as well as the future. The term *meek* has its roots in the Hebrew word *anawin*, which was used as a synonym for "poor" opposite of rich and domineering. Too often we associate *meek* with weak, harmless, or timid. Nothing could be more foreign to the biblical use of the word *meek*. Rather it carries with it a sense of strength that comes out of being humble, teachable, and in tune with God. It is the opposite of being proud, arrogant, and closed.

This beatitude is a close parallel to Psalm 37:11: "But the meek shall inherit the land, and delight themselves in abundant prosperity." It is important to observe the phrases "will inherit the earth" or "inherit the land" and think about how right relationships and attitudes affect our relationship with the earth.

The word *meek* is used elsewhere in scripture to describe Moses (Numbers 12:3) and Jesus (Matthew 11:29). Moses defied the might of Egypt and Jesus stood up to the powers of Rome and local religious authorities. Both were fearless in the face of powerful systems. Both stood up for justice, mercy and truth at the risk of death. Meekness has a mysterious strength that baffles the high and mighty of this world. Meekness leads to prosperity for all, not a select few.

Discuss as a group.

■ Moses and Jesus were called meek. What have you learned about Moses and Jesus that would counter the popular notion that meekness is weakness or timidity?

■ A number of meanings are given to the word *meek*. Which of the following are most helpful to you? How?

   a. One who has control of his or her instincts, impulses, and passions.
   b. A humility that banishes pride and allows one to be teachable.
   c. A compassionate use of one's strengths to help others.

d. One who does not need to always be in control or always win.

e. A gentleness (non-violence) that promotes harmony with others and the earth.

f. A sense of awe and gratitude toward the works and mystery of God.

g. Other.

■ Choose one of the above descriptions and tell of an example of this that you have witnessed or read about. It could be an individual or group. What blessings resulted?

■ Certain attitudes in society are inconsistent with a biblical understanding of meekness. Choose the one you have struggled with the most and tell about your struggle.

a. Technology is our salvation, our priority.
b. Competition is needed for growth/progress.
c. Meekness is not a sign of strength for men.
d. Meekness is not a sign of strength for women.
e. A need to win and be in control.
f. Silence is seen as weakness or inferiority.
g. Religion belittles knowledge.
h. Little encouragement to learn from the environment or lack of connectedness to creation.
i. Other.

Discuss as a group.

Consider this

Environmental degradation is threatening our survival on this planet. The human impact on the biosphere has brought about a deterioration of God's creation. Trends are discouraging as we trace the factors of atmospheric pollution, land use, water quality and quantity, extinction of species, loss of ozone, and population growth. Al Gore, vice president of the United States and an active leader in environmental concerns, has called for a "Global Marshall Plan." He said, "If we cannot embrace the preservation of the earth as our new organizing principle, the very survival of our civilization will be in doubt."

From *Earth in the Balance: Ecology and the Human Spirit* (New York: Houghton Mifflin, 1992).

- Learning takes discipline. Give examples of how has this been true in your life.

- What opportunities for learning has the church offered that have helped you the most? What more might be done? How does learning about global issues teach meekness?

- What could we do to teach our children about the blessings of meekness?

Explore and relate.

- (Optional.) Share with the group an experience you have had when the need to control or win was so overpowering that you felt manipulated or abused. Do this without using names or being judgmental. It could be the story of an institutional system, a tradition, or an accepted attitude. What did you learn from it?

A further look

Read Numbers 12 and Ephesians 4:1-3.

- What do these texts suggest for our relationships with one another?

- What kind of personal character is associated with a biblical understanding of meekness (humility)?

Discovery

Exodus 2:11-22

Optional: Assign parts for dramatic reading of this text.

11 One day, after Moses had grown up, he went out to his people and saw their forced labor. He saw an Egyptian beating a Hebrew, one of his kinsfolk. 12He looked this way and that, and seeing no one he killed the Egyptian and hid him in the sand. 13When he went out the next day, he saw two Hebrews fighting; and he said to the one who was in the wrong, "Why do you strike your fellow Hebrew?" 14He answered, "Who made you a ruler and judge over us? Do you mean to kill me as you killed the Egyptian?" Then Moses was afraid and thought, "Surely the thing is known." 15When Pharaoh heard of it, he sought to kill Moses. But Moses fled from Pharaoh. He settled in the land of Midian, and sat down by a well. 1CThe priest of Midian had seven daughters. They came to draw water, and filled the troughs to water their father's flock. 17But some shepherds came and drove them away. Moses got up and came to their defense and watered their flock. 18When they returned to their father Reuel, he

said, "How is it that you have come back so soon today?" [19]They said, "An Egyptian helped us against the shepherds; he even drew water for us and watered the flock." [20]He said to his daughters, "Where is he? Why did you leave the man? Invite him to break bread." [21]Moses agreed to stay with the man, and he gave Moses his daughter Zipporah in marriage. [22]She bore a son, and he named him Gershom; for he said, "I have been an alien residing in a foreign land."

Moses in Egypt

A review of what preceded this part of the exodus story is helpful. Remember the new king in Egypt who "did not know Joseph" (Exodus 1:8)? He was not sympathetic toward the Hebrews living in northern Egypt. He put into place a government policy calling for the death of Hebrew baby boys and forced the Hebrew people to provide cheap labor for the Egyptian economy. Moses was born and brought into the palace because Pharaoh's daughter wanted to adopt him. Moses' mother became his nanny (nurse). While the Hebrews' lives were made bitter under repressive laws and biased propaganda, Moses grew into adulthood, living in the comforts of the Pharaoh's home.

Our text begins with Moses leaving the palace to see for himself what was happening. His face-to-face encounter with oppression and suffering stirred up anger within him. His first reaction was to strike out in violence and kill an Egyptian. Moses fled to Midian, a neighboring country, where he later had his burning bush experience. Our concentration will be focused on the learning opportunities given to Moses that helped prepare him for the responsibility of leadership.

Discuss as a group.

- Study the text and pool your observations about the various learning opportunities Moses had. Use your imagination. What learning opportunities might Moses have had growing up in the palace with his mother as his nanny?

- Moses killed a man. He was criticized by fellow Hebrews. Soon he had to flee for his life. Share with the group something you have learned through your mistakes and failures.

- Moses learned some things through a face-to-face encounter, things that are not learned as well by just hearing or reading about it (see Exodus 2:11). He saw the suffering firsthand. Think of a situation where you have learned about something experientially and share the experience, including your feelings, with the group.

■ Of the four following statements, pick the one that best fits you right now and tell why.

> a. I didn't develop a social conscience (sensitivity toward social injustice and suffering) until I left my palace environment and went out to see what was going on. It happened when . . .
>
> b. I have difficulty with the sight of suffering, such as pictures of hungry children or dead bodies. I respond better to happy faces and signs of hope.
>
> c. I wish our whole educational system would be more open to experiential learning and not so tied to the classroom and textbooks.
>
> d. Like Moses, I have trouble with my feelings of anger and impatience when I see so much suffering around me. The place of my "Midian escape" is . . .

■ Perhaps Moses learned to be open and teachable from his mother, or from his father-in-law, or from experiences. From what persons or experiences have you learned this attitude?

Consider this

"What is the test that you have indeed undergone this holy birth? Listen carefully. If this birth has taken place within you, then every single creature points you toward God."

—Maister Eckhart

■ What discipline would you like to have or strengthen that would help you be more conscious of God's presence in the midst of daily life?

Community building through our actions

Discuss as a group.

Have each person in the group consider one of the following things to do as a way of entering more fully into the meaning of the text for this theme.

■ Volunteer to help in some social service agency that will give you a face-to-face encounter with a segment of society that is hurting.

■ Set aside time to get closer to nature. Find out what it can teach you about meekness.

- Make a list of all the opposites to meekness that you see encouraged through advertising in one week. Share and discuss it with someone.

- Talk to an educator about the value she or he sees in experiential learning. Find out ways this is encouraged today. Offer encouragement and support.

- Plan a trip to a third-world situation (near you or in another country) and see what it teaches you about meekness. Or go listen to someone who has just returned from such an experience.

- Write a note of thanks to someone who has modeled for you or taught you to be open and willing to learn.

- Pick an area where you feel you are in need of meekness, an area you need to be more open and teachable. Decide on steps you will take to improve your attitude.

- Write a Christian environmentalist creed. Read it to the group next week.

A further look

Discuss as a group.

The Eighth Beatitude deals with persecution and resistance when the values of the kingdom are lived out.

- Look up these verses and discuss how this is true for you and what it says about meekness (being teachable).

    a. John 17:14-17 — The world has hated them.
    b. Amos 7:10-15 — Amos was told to keep his mouth shut.

Wrap-up

Before you go, take time for the following:

- Group ministry task

- Review

- Personal concerns and prayer concerns

- Closing prayers

Daily walk

Bible readings

Day 1 Titus 3:2
Call to be gentle.

Day 2 Micah 6:8
Do justice, love, kindness, walk humbly.

Day 3 Numbers 12:1-3
Meekness in the face of criticism.

Day 4 Phil. 2:1-5
Look to the interests of others.

Day 5 2 Cor. 10:1-5
Appeal to meekness and what brings about spiritual gentleness.

Day 6 Genesis 1:26-31
Called to tenderly care for creation.

Day 7 2 Chron. 7:14
Renewal.

Thought for the journey

Meekness comes when we connect with nature and each other in such a way that we see the sacredness in everything God created. Take time to connect.

Prayer for the journey

Gracious God, help us to be so in tune with your Word and your world that we are eager to learn and gentle in how we treat others and your creation.

Verse for the journey

"Come to me, all you that are weary and are carrying heavy burdens, and I will give you rest. Take my yoke upon you, and learn from me, for I am gentle and humble in heart, and you will find rest for your souls" (Matthew 11:28-29).

Empowerment for Living

Focus

Learning to focus our lives on God's will (justice and righteousness) empowers us to say both yes and no at appropriate moments, thereby discovering a satisfaction the world cannot give.

Community building

Option

Tell about a time you wanted something intensely and what you did about it.

■ House inventory. Using the grading scale below, take an inventory of your own life by giving yourself a grade on how you feel you are doing in each "room." Share with the group your best and worst grades and explain them.

(A = satisfied; B = making improvement; C = needs adjustment; D = needs major improvement.)

____ Library (mind): Learning, pursuing, understanding.
____ Dining room (body): taking care of your body, eating the proper foods, and meeting physical needs.
____ Workshop (action): Using your gifts and talents, your work, to contribute to society and the world, whether for pay or as a volunteer.
____ Family room (community): Spending time with loved ones, giving support, sharing feelings, and listening.
____ Recreation room (fun): Letting the child in you come out, relaxing, playing, laughing, and celebrating life.
____ Hall closet (hidden things): Where you stash things that are neglected or hard to deal with; guilty feelings.
____ Bedroom (intimacy): Where you develop close relationships, build friendship, experience the power of touch, and enjoy human sexuality.
____ Foyer (the welcoming place): Being hospitable to new people and experiences; enjoying community.

Discovery

Matthew 5:6

Read aloud and respond as a group.

6 **"Blessed are those who hunger and thirst for righteousness, for they will be filled."**

The Fourth Beatitude

The Fourth Beatitude connects us to the Old Testament concept of justice. The word *righteousness* can also be translated "justice," which means the reordering of relationships, bringing back into harmony, and restoring wholeness and community. Justice is the activity of God to change both the hearts of people and the systems of society that have turned away from God's intention.

In the Hebrew scripture, justice was always looked upon as central to messianic hope (the coming of the anointed king who would bring God's reign of peace) as expressed in Jeremiah 23:5-6: "The days are surely coming, says the LORD, when I will raise up for David a righteous Branch, and he shall reign as king and deal wisely, and shall execute justice and righteousness in the land. In his days Judah will be saved and Israel will live in safety. And this is the name by which he will be called: 'The LORD is our righteousness.'"

In the life of Jesus we see what God's justice (righteousness) is about. It is a radical kind of compassion, an unconventional wisdom, a hunger and thirst for equality and dignity based on the unique worth of every human being. It is a commitment to solidarity and sacrifice for people who are lost and hurting. God's justice is both courageous and costly. To live this justice (righteousness), one needs to continually experience God's grace, follow Jesus, and believe in him. Notice Jesus does not say "Blessed are those who achieve justice," but "Blessed are those who hunger and thirst for it."

Matthew's immediate audience lived in an arid country. They knew what intense hunger and thirst were like. When there is no water or no food, one's attention and activity become extremely focused.

- Share the memory of a time when you were hungry or "dying of thirst" (figuratively). What did you do?

- Were there side effects?

- If nothing comes to mind, tell about a movie or book where it was so.

This beatitude uses two basic physical needs (hunger and thirst) to describe what is important in the experience of happiness and harmony (blessedness).

- Which of the following do you think best fits the idea of hunger and thirst?

Choose one and explain.

  a. Letting go of putting self first and centering on others.
  b. Wanting to do God's will so intensely that all of life has a single focus.
  c. A strong desire to learn God's word in order to know what God's agenda is.
  d. Becoming able to see beyond charity and working for justice or a change in the economic or political order.
  e. Wanting to see change so strongly that you are willing to sacrifice as Jesus did.
  f. Experiencing a profound emptiness and humility that opens one up to what God has to offer.
  g. Other.

- Of the following, check the three that you feel have influenced (programmed) you most in determining what you should hunger and thirst for in life. Also note the one that has had the least influence. Explain.

a. Advertising	e. Peer pressure	i. Movies
b. Education	f. Heroes	j. Greed
c. News media	g. Appetites	k. History
d. Religion	h. Success	l. Tradition

- Hum or whistle an advertising tune and see if people can guess what ad it comes from.

- If we were to follow this advertising, what would we hunger and thirst for?

- What are the evidences of the influence of advertising?

- After telling the disciples not to worry about what to eat, drink, and wear, and not to worry about tomorrow, Jesus said, "Strive first for the kingdom of God and its righteousness (justice), and all these things will be given to you as well" (Matthew 6:33). How does this verse speak to you in your walk with God? How does it relate to the Fourth Beatitude? Does it raise questions for you?

■ Choose one of the following events in the life and message of Jesus and share what you think it says about the righteousness (justice) of God.

    a. The birth of Jesus (God becoming flesh).
    b. Jesus' healing ministry.
    c. Washing the disciples' feet.
    d. "I desire mercy, not sacrifice."
    e. The story of the Good Samaritan: "Go do likewise."
    f. Jesus' death and resurrection.
    g. Jesus ate with tax collectors, prostitutes, and sinners.
    h. The story of the prodigal son and his elder brother.
    i. "Whoever does not receive the kingdom of God as a little child will never enter it."

■ What has helped you recently to become more focused on the justice (righteousness) of God? Choose one of the following and tell about it to the group.

    a. Example of someone.
    b. Prayer/solitude.
    c. A personal experience.
    d. Preaching/teaching.
    e. Small group discussion.
    f. Getting involved.
    g. Public worship.
    h. Other.

Exodus 1:13-21

Read aloud and discuss
as a group.

13 The Egyptians became ruthless in imposing tasks on the Israelites, 14and made their lives bitter with hard service in mortar and brick and in every kind of field labor. They were ruthless in all the tasks that they imposed on them. 15The king of Egypt said to the Hebrew midwives, one of whom was named Shiphrah and the other Puah, 16"When you act as midwives to the Hebrew women, and see them on the birthstool, if it is a boy, kill him; but if it is a girl, she shall live." 17But the midwives feared God; they did not do as the king of Egypt commanded them, but they let the boys live. 18So the king of Egypt summoned the midwives and said to them, "Why have you done this, and allowed the boys to live?" 19The midwives said to Pharaoh, "Because the Hebrew women are not like the Egyptian women; for they are vigorous and give birth before the midwife comes to them." 20So God dealt well with the midwives; and the people multiplied and became very strong. 21And because the midwives feared God, he gave them families.

Shiphrah and Puah follow their conscience

Exodus 1:8 tells us that a new king was in power in Egypt. This new administration took a different path toward the Hebrew people, one of dominance and violence. The Hebrews were made to labor as slaves. They were made to suffer in the name of national security (1:9-10). The rationale given to the people was that it was necessary for the future safety and stability of the country. The king appealed to their sense of nationalism, patriotism, and economic prosperity.

The story of the midwives, Shiphrah and Puah, is one of the first examples of civil disobedience in the Bible. The two women followed their conscience rather than obey the law of the land. They risked their lives in order to save the lives of children because they feared God. Many times we find that women were the ones who had courage to resist evil or venture out in faith in obedience to God's will.

■ The Egyptians made the Hebrews' lives bitter with hard service. Share with the group examples of lives being made bitter with hard service and ruthlessness in today's world.

- ■ (Optional.) Do you think women are more apt to act compassionately toward human suffering than men? Why have we heard so little about Shiphrah and Puah?

- ■ Violence is often done by systems in control, by institutions or powers or unjust laws. Discuss institutional violence and how it manifests itself today—that is, how people are hurt by systems of domination, power over others, and greed. Areas to consider might be racism, sexism, nationalism, ageism, and corporate greed.

- ■ If you had been one of the midwives in this story and were approached to join the others in refusing to obey the law to kill the Hebrew males at birth, what do you think your response would have been? (Choose one or two of the following and explain.)

    a. Wanted a lot of time to think about it because . . .
    b. Agreed to join the midwives, but still afraid.
    c. Argued that it is not right to disobey governing authority.
    d. Thought, "What's the use? It won't work."
    e. Found an excuse or a way to avoid the issue.
    f. Said no but would pray for them.
    g. Said yes because of compassion for children.
    h. Did not want to be labeled a social activist.
    i. Other.

- ■ How can one know when to refuse to follow what society or institutions ask of us, whether in the form of established laws, codes of behavior, or societal expectations? Can you give an example of when you had to make such a decision?

Explore and relate. ■ Tell about a time when you were treated unjustly. How did it feel? What did you do?

Discovery

Matthew 5:10

10 "Blessed are those who are persecuted for righteousness' (justice's) sake, for theirs is the kingdom of heaven."

- ■ How did the powers of domination and violence (both religious and secular) seek to destroy the mission and message of Jesus?

- ■ How is it done today? What tactics are used?

- Who has inspired you by their willingness to suffer for the sake of justice?

- Sing together the simple tune from Taize, "Ubi Caritas," printed below.

- Jesus once said, "I have not come to bring peace, but a sword" (Matthew 10:34b). Who do you think he meant?

A further look

Read texts aloud and answer as a group.

Read Luke 10:38-42 and Acts 10:1-35.

- Discuss how Mary, Peter, and Cornelius had to break with tradition in order to seek out the truth.

- What traditions have you had to question in your hunger and thirst for righteousness and justice?

- Before continuing with — or as a part of — "Wrap-up," consider reading 1 John 4:7 and singing "Ubi Caritas."

Wrap-up

Before you go, take time for the following:

- Group ministry task

- Review

- Personal concerns and prayer concerns

- Closing prayers

Daily walk

Bible readings

Day 1 Luke 4:18-19
Jesus' mission to the world.

Day 2 Matthew 23:23
Justice, a weightier matter.

Day 3 Psalm 72:1-4
Justice and the poor.

Day 4 Isaiah 58:6-10
The "fast" God chooses.

Day 5 Jer. 22:15-16
To know God is to do justice.

Day 6 Amos 5:21-24
Let justice roll like rivers.

Day 7 Luke 6:46-49
Laying a good foundation.

Thought for the journey

We have no mission but to serve
In full obedience to our Lord;
To care for all, without reserve,
And spread his liberating Word.

Prayer for the journey

Lord, help us to do justice, love kindness, and walk humbly with you. Amen.

Verse for the journey

"Beloved, let us love one another, because love is from God; everyone who loves is born of God and knows God" (1 John 4:7).

5 When Hurt and Hope Embrace

To learn what it means to be compassionate in a hurting world and find steps to bring hope and healing to victims of violence, greed, and domination.

Community building

Option

In groups of two (or three, if necessary) let each person respond to one of the three directives listed at right. After the speaker has shared, the listener(s) will tell what he or she heard the other person say (both the content and feelings expressed). The conversation is completed once the speaker is confident that the listener(s) understood what the speaker intended. Once the process is complete, reverse speaker and listener roles.

With the entire small group, tell what it was like to be a part of such attentive conversation.

■ Think about this past week or two. Tell the group what you would like them to know about your recent life experiences. See this opportunity as a gift to you and the group. What surprises have you experienced? What new people have you met? Where have you sensed the presence of God?

■ Tell about a time in your life when things looked rather hopeless for you and you were ready to give up. What were the circumstances? What helped to bring you through it?

■ Imagine that you were given a private audience with Jesus today. You have the opportunity to ask him one question. What would that question be? Explain the question's importance to you.

Opening prayer

God of grace and God of glory, on your people pour your power. Breathe into us the fresh wind of the Holy Spirit. As we gather around your Word make us more aware of your world so that we might bring hope where there is hurt. Amen.

Matthew 5:7,9

[7] "Blessed are the merciful, for they will receive mercy. . . . [9] Blessed are the peacemakers, for they will be called children of God."

Mercy and compassion

Read aloud.

These two beatitudes both relate to compassion, attitude, and action.

For Matthew, *mercy* is a broad term that includes an attitude of forgiveness and compassion. There is both a critique and an exhortation in Jesus' quote from the Old Testament: "I desire mercy, not sacrifice" (Matthew 9:13). A religion centered in sacrifice may neglect the necessary acts of compassion toward the world while concentrating on proper acts of worship and personal piety.

Compassion embraces the meaning of both mercy and peacemaking. The Hebrew word for compassion is derived from the word meaning *womb*. Womb love is a deep feeling with relational power that comes from the center of our being. It is a way of being that flows out from an intimate feeling of oneness. *Compassion* in Latin means "to suffer with." Henri Nouwen reminds us that it calls forth a willingness to go where it hurts, enter into places of pain, and share in brokenness and fear. It is important to keep in mind that both mercy and compassion begin with an attitude that is not paternalistic or condescending. It does not begin from a position of privilege or superiority. God, who is compassionate, is one who cares deeply, who gives new life, and enters into solidarity with all who suffer.

Discuss as a group.

- Think of an example where charity and help were given to someone in need, but from a superior and paternalistic stance. What are the long-term effects of this attitude of giving?

- When Jesus quoted from the Old Testament and said, "I desire mercy, not sacrifice," what do you think he meant? How can we apply it? Choose one of the following and explain or give an example.

    a. How we live during the week is more important than coming to worship on Sunday.
    b. Rules can get in the way of genuine love.
    c. The Old Testament shedding of blood for sins (atonement) was no longer necessary in Jesus' theology.

d. We should stress right attitudes more than right behavior or right beliefs.
e. Stop all your hypocrisy.
f. We learn from Jesus how to be compassionate, not
what kind of offerings to give.
g. Maybe we stress right forms of worship/liturgy/
creeds at the expense of caring for people.
h. Other.

■ The Seventh Beatitude encourages us to be peacemakers,
not peace lovers. Tell about someone who has inspired
you by their peacemaking efforts. What have they done?
What are the results?

■ The compassion demonstrated in Jesus' life was radical
and different to many in his day. Choose one of the following and suggest how it may have surprised or star-
tled his contemporaries or our society. In what way was
it radical or different?

You may wish to look
up one or more of these
Bible passages for ex-
amples of Jesus' views
on these subjects.

a. Jesus' teaching about praying for enemies (Luke
6:27-32).
b. Jesus' attitude toward children (Mark 10:13-16).
c. Jesus' attitude toward women (John 4:27-30).
d. Jesus' attitude toward the poor (Mark 10:17-22;
Luke 14:21).
e. Jesus' teaching about forgiveness (Matthew 18:21-
22).
f. Jesus' attitude toward status and honor (Matthew
19:30; John 13:12-15).

Read aloud.

Consider this

**Arnold, who has made his no-questions-asked peace with
the world for $30,000 a year, speaks to his ne'er-do-well
brother Murray, who has rebelled against the deceits of
conventional society and cares about people passionately.**

**I have long been aware, Murray. . . . I have long been
aware that you don't respect me much. I suppose there
are a lot of brothers who don't get along. . . . Unfortu-
nately for you, Murray, you want to be a hero. Maybe if
a fella falls into a lake, you can jump in and save him;
there's still that kind of stuff. But who gets opportunities like that in midtown Manhattan, with all that traffic?
I am willing to deal with the available world and I do not
choose to shake it up but to live with it. There's the people who spill things, and the people who get spilled on; I
do not choose to notice the stains, Murray. I have a wife
and two children, and business, like they say, is business.**

I am not an exceptional man, so it is possible for me to stay with things the way they are. I'm lucky, I'm gifted; I have a talent for surrender. I'm at peace. But you are cursed, and I like you, so it makes me sad, you don't have the gift; and I see the torture of it. All I can do is worry for you. But I will not worry for myself; you cannot convince me that I am one of the Bad Guys. I get up, I go, I lie a little, I peddle a little, I watch the rules, I talk the talk. We fellas have those offices high up there so we can catch the wind and go with it, however it blows. But, and I will not apologize for it, I take pride; I am the best possible Arnold Burns.

From "I Am Not an Exceptional Man" by Herb Gardner. Quoted in *Creative Brooding* by Robert A. Raines (New York: Macmillan, 1966), 17.

Discuss as a group.

■ How do you respond to this man's reasoning?

■ What would you say to him?

■ Who is getting spilled on? What do these two beatitudes say to this situation?

Discovery

Exodus 3:7-10

7 Then the LORD said, "I have observed the misery of my people who are in Egypt; I have heard their cry on account of their taskmasters. Indeed, I know their sufferings, 8and I have come down to deliver them from the Egyptians, and to bring them up out of that land to a good and broad land, a land flowing with milk and honey, to the country of the Canaanites, the Hittites, the Amorites, the Perizzites, the Hivites, and the Jebusites. 9The cry of the Israelites has now come to me; I have also seen how the Egyptians oppress them. 10So come, I will send you to Pharaoh to bring my people, the Israelites, out of Egypt.

God sends Moses to liberate the Hebrews

This passage is part of God's speech to Moses in the burning bush experience. Moses was prepared to hear this only after his spiritual awareness of the presence of God. Sometimes we don't hear things because we're not ready.

Notice in 3:7 that God observes misery, God hears the cries of the afflicted, and God knows about their suffering. God is not detached from the human predicament. It is as though God is suffering with them.

God acted to liberate the Hebrews by sending Moses to Pharaoh. Moses was not asked to go to Goshen in Egypt where the suffering was being experienced.

Instead Moses was sent to the seat of political power where the decisions were being made that caused the suffering. Moses was called to confront the principalities and powers, to get involved in politics. It was no easy task.

Discuss as a group. Share an example of hope being given to a group of people suffering today.

> ■ In what way is the church enabling hurt and hope to embrace?

Being compassionate and working for peace can put us into contact with injustice and violence. We may be confronted with principalities and powers—within and around us—that are causing hurt and hopelessness (Ephesians 6:12).

> ■ How do you respond when this seems to happen as you are trying to be compassionate (with family and friends, coworkers, school, church, or the larger world of politics)?

Choose one and explain.
> a. I am uncomfortable with any activity.
> b. I have never noticed that Moses was called by God to confront the politics/power in Egypt. I find this scary and/or encouraging because . . .
> c. If our hearts are transformed by the Holy Spirit, then the world will change. Let's stick to changing people's hearts because . . .
> d. I really struggle with this because . . .
> e. Other.

Before we are prepared to go to the Pharaohs of today on behalf of the victims of injustice, we need to listen to their cries, know about their suffering, and feel with them.

> ■ What has been the best way you have found to listen, to see, and to suffer with the victims of violence, greed, and dominance?
>
> > a. From announcements and prayers in church.
> > b. By reading about it in the news media.
> > c. By meeting people who have been there.

d. By face-to-face encounters with victims.
e. By reading the Bible.
f. By opening my home to refugees or victims.
g. By observing effects of corporate decisions.
h. By being in tune with violence in myself.
i. Other.

■ What might be a first or next step for you in becoming more involved in peacemaking?

Choose one or two of the following and share your plans with the group.

a. Pray for a change in attitude toward social justice ministry.
b. Write a letter to an elected leader.
c. Get into a group or organization that is involved in peacemaking.
d. Study what the Bible says about non-violence and doing justice.
e. Balance my inward and outward journey.
f. Be intentional in having a face-to-face encounter with victims.
g. Read a good book that opens up the issues.
h. Give more generously to the needs of others.
i. Be more attentive to the needs and hurts of those around me.

■ Form groups of three and, with a large piece of paper and crayons or colored pencils, create a picture or feeling of compassion. Let the others in your group tell you what they see and feel. Then give your interpretation.

Consider this

"What if a group of South African women in a squatters' village suddenly find themselves set upon by soldiers and bulldozers and are told they have two minutes to clear out. Shall they get guns and protect themselves? There are none. And most of the men are away at work. Here is what they did. Knowing how puritanical rural white Dutch Reformed Afrikaners can be, the black women stood in front of the bulldozers and stripped off all their clothes. The police turned tail and fled. . ."

From *Engaging the Powers* by Walter Wink, copyright © 1992 Fortress Press.

"To make any progress we must not make speeches and organize mass meetings but be prepared for mountains of suffering."

From *Gandhi's Truth: On the Origins of Militant Non-violence* by Mahatma Gandhi (New York: Norton, 1969).

A further look

Read texts aloud and answer as a group.

Read Isaiah 1:17 and Romans 12:9-21.

- Which of the things listed in the Romans passage do you most want to work on in your own life?
- Which cause the most resistance in today's society?
- Rewrite Isaiah 1:17 in language young teens would use.

Wrap-up

Before you go, take time for the following:

- Group ministry task

- Review

- Personal concerns and prayer concerns

- Closing prayers

Daily walk

Bible readings

Day 1   Luke 19:1-10
Reparations to the poor.

Day 2   Luke 19:41-44
Palm Sunday peace march.

Day 3   Luke 6:36
Be merciful (compassionate).

Day 4   Luke 1:46-53
*Mary's song about
compassion.*

Day 5   Matt. 25:36-46
What's the bottom line?

Day 6   Acts 8:26-40
Compassion for outcasts.

Day 7   Matt. 10:36-46
Peace may include conflict.

Thought for the journey

My own journey has led beyond belief (and beyond doubt and disbelief) to an understanding of the Christian life as a relationship to the Spirit of God, a relationship that involves one in a journey of transformation.

From *Meeting Jesus Again for the First Time* by Marcus J. Borg (New York: HarperCollins, 1994), 17.

Prayer for the journey

God, make us discontent with things the way they are in this world of violence and fear. Jar our complacence, expose our excuses and inspire us to be peacemakers. Amen.

Verse for the journey

Save us from weak resignation
To the evils we deplore;
Let the gift of your salvation
Be our glory evermore.
Grant us wisdom, grant us courage,
Serving you whom we adore,
Serving you whom we adore.

6 Learning Balance in My Growth

Focus

To learn how change, balance, and singleness of heart are part of the faith journey as we develop and grow in Christ.

Community building

Option

Observe the picture below. Do you see the older woman? A younger woman? Both? Which did you see first? Think of a time when your perception of something changed. Share your experience.

- Divide into pairs and tell about a time when you tried learning (doing) something new and different, like skiing, speaking a new language, golf, dieting, using a computer, praying in public, being retired, or being a parent. Share your struggles and what helped you.

- (Optional.) After three to five minutes, gather as a group and ask each person to summarize what his or her partner described.

- In groups of three or four, share with each other how you have changed your thinking, behavior, or feelings in one of the areas listed below. What initiated the change? Has the change been a blessing, a burden, or a challenge?

  a. Music you enjoy
  b. Sports participation
  c. Food you eat
  d. Your world view
  e. Your view of nature
  f. Prayer

  g. Friendship
  h. Medicine
  i. Violence
  j. Money
  k. Religion
  l. Other

Opening prayer

Gracious God, forgive what we have been. Correct what we are, and order what we shall be, for thy sake and ours, through Jesus Christ our Lord. Amen.

Matthew 5:8

8 **"Blessed are the pure in heart, for they will see God."**

The Sixth Beatitude

Soren Kierkegaard, a nineteenth-century Danish philosopher, wrote a book entitled, "Purity of Heart Is to Will One Thing." The title suggests the essential meaning of this beatitude.

Our understanding of each beatitude has been enlightened by a closer look at what Jesus taught and did as recorded in the gospels. Never did Jesus expect perfection or sinlessness. The pure in heart are those who have let go of conflicting loyalties and experienced singleness of heart.

From Jesus we learn that one cannot serve two masters. Jesus exposed hypocrisy and was critical of those who said one thing but lived something else. Learning to will one thing involves a dying to old and harmful allegiances or values. Jesus described this when he said, "unless a grain of wheat falls into the earth and dies, it remains just a single grain; but if it dies, it bears much fruit" (John 12:24). In Matthew 16:25 Jesus said, "Those who want to save their life will lose it, and those who lose their life for my sake will find it."

In our study of this beatitude we will focus on what it means to be open to newness and change as we experience that continuous death and resurrection that Jesus talked about.

Explore and relate.

■ As you look back on your own growth from your birth, what stage of life did you find most difficult? What made you aware that change, for example, physical, mental, emotional, social, or beliefs/values, was happening?

Discuss as a group.

■ Jesus talked about the grain of wheat falling to the ground and dying . . . and about willing to lose one's life to find it. What experience have you had where you found you needed to let go of something in order to give attention to something more important? How was it a struggle, a freeing experience, a growth experience?

■ How do you feel about religious hypocrisy (saying one thing but living something different—lacking a singleness of heart) as you see it in others? In yourself?

■ Purity of heart involves a life-long journey with the living God to find meaning and wholeness. One's spiritual growth is a search for identity, integrity, and singleness of heart. The following is a list of stages or growth experiences many Christians encounter to some degree.

After each definition is read aloud and discussed for clarifications, mark an X on the continuum to designate the degree to which you see yourself motivated by the grace of God to explore and develop this area of your life. A 1 indicates little interest, a 5 indicates extreme interest. The group may wish to share individual responses in the seven categories as a whole or in groups of three or four.

There is no proper order to them, nor is this list descriptive of everyone's journey. Many people discover they may go back and forth among these areas and others, and that a balance is important. They are listed here to engage our thinking about the importance of being open to change and growth, and to strive for the balance and wholeness toward which the Beatitudes point.

a. Grace and forgiveness
The awakening of the heart toward God; being amazed at God's love and acceptance, without strings attached; feeling unworthy but forgiven; given a new start; discovering the meaning of grace.

1	2	3	4	5

b. Decision and discipline
Responding to Jesus' invitation to follow him, not just believing a set of doctrines; realizing there is a "yes" as well as "no" in the life of discipleship; being Christian requires commitment and letting go.

1	2	3	4	5

c. The journey inward and prayer
Desire to know the Bible and becoming more intimate with Jesus; developing a personal prayer life; contemplation and reflection on spiritual issues.

1	2	3	4	5

d. Community and connectedness
Sensing the importance and need for fellowship and encouragement from other Christians; learning to share faith stories and admit one's struggles and joys; embracing the global family of God and God's creation.

1	2	3	4	5

e. Questioning and exploring

More aware of the church's weaknesses and that not everything has absolute answers; facing doubts about one's experiences and what others say one should believe; exploring alternative views and interpretations of the Bible.

1	2	3	4	5

f. The journey outward and compassion

Wanting to get involved in meaningful relationships and learning how to love one's neighbors; a growing sense of the radical nature of Jesus' message and the centrality of compassion and justice toward the poor and oppressed.

1	2	3	4	5

g. Empowerment and mission

An openness to the presence and power of the Holy Spirit in one's life; a desire to know what one's gifts might be; a growing appreciation of God's intervention and the place of healing in the church's life; wanting to be in partnership in ministry with others through the guidance of the Holy Spirit.

1	2	3	4	5

■ Which area of your faith journey do you see yourself wanting to explore the most? What do you think you will find? What is the first step you will need to take?

■ As you take your first step, what are the perils and pitfalls to guard against?

■ Share an experience you have had in exploring a new area of spiritual growth and change.

The Beatitudes in perspective and for review

Beatitude	Attitude	Promise
Blessed are the poor in Spirit	Open to spiritual discoveries	Theirs is the kingdom of heaven
Blessed are those who mourn	Embrace the darkness, capacity to grieve	They will be comforted
Blessed are the meek	Being teachable	They will inherit the earth
Blessed are those who hunger and thirst for for righteousness	Strong desire to correct injustice, restore harmony	They will be filled
Blessed are the merciful	Sharing the pain of others	They will receive mercy
Blessed are the pure in heart	Singleness of heart	They will see God
Blessed are the peacemakers	Compassion for reconciliation and peace	They will be called children of God
Blessed are those who are persecuted for righteousness' sake	Accepting the cost of discipleship	Theirs is the kingdom of God

■ Choose one of the beatitudes that has opened up for you in a new way or challenged your thinking. Share your discovery with the group.

■ Rate the Beatitudes in the order of how you see your response to their challenge — growth in discipleship — with 1 being most responsive and 8 being the least responsive. Share your No. 1 and No. 8 beatitudes with the group.

Consider using these prayers as part of "Wrap-up."

■ Write in the space below a prayer that expresses your desire for God's guidance as you seek to make the attitudes of the Beatitudes a part of your spiritual journey.

Discovery

Exodus 2:5-10

5 The daughter of Pharaoh came down to bathe at the river, while her attendants walked beside the river. She saw the basket among the reeds and sent her maid to bring it. 6When she opened it, she saw the child. He was crying, and she took pity on him, "This must be one of the Hebrews' children," she said. 7Then his sister said to Pharaoh's daughter, "Shall I go and get you a nurse from the Hebrew women to nurse the child for you?" 8Pharaoh's daughter said to her, "Yes." So the girl went and called the child's mother. 9Pharaoh's daughter said to her, "Take this child and nurse it for me, and I will give you your wages." So the woman took the child and nursed it. 10When the child grew up, she brought him to Pharaoh's daughter, and she took him as her son. She named him Moses, "because," she said, "I drew him out of the water."

The women rescue Moses

The daughter of Pharaoh most likely was fully aware of the public policy toward the Hebrews and especially their baby boys. There may have been frequent conversations about it at the dinner table. Pharaoh was her father. It was a law that required the death of Hebrew babies. Her action took great courage.

It appears that Moses' sister and mother were not far away. At the right moment Moses' sister came forth and offered to find a nanny, who turned out to be Moses' mother. Evidently their faith prompted them to take a calculated risk. They didn't sit back and accept fate. They made a basket and then waited for an opportunity to do something. They were proactive.

- In a moment of crisis, just a short distance away was Miriam, Moses' sister. Think of a time when you needed a sister or brother, or when you were a sister or brother to someone. Tell about it.

- Pharaoh's daughter had to make a decision. It was a decision that involved both a "yes" and a "no." What did the "no" involve? What did the "yes" involve? Where do you see singleness of heart?

- What "yes" and what "no" have been part of your willingness to lose your life in order to find life?

- What "yes" and "no" do you face at the present time?

- Share how this study of the Beatitudes and the story of Moses has both encouraged you and challenged you.

A further look

Read texts aloud and answer as a group.

Read John 3:1-10; John 4:7-26; Mark 10:17-22; and Mark 10:46-52.

- Discuss how Jesus dealt differently with different people. What is the bottom line? What is essential?

- Share how you have appreciated the various stories of how people have encountered Christ.

Wrap-up

Before you go, take time for the following:

- Group ministry task

- Review

- Personal concerns and prayer concerns

- Closing prayers

Daily walk

Bible readings

Day 1 Psalm 24
Clean hands and pure heart.

Day 2 Psalm 1
Planted by streams of water.

Day 3 Luke 10:38-42
One thing is needful.

Day 4 Jer. 29:11-14
If with all your heart.

Day 5 Matt.6:25-26
Lose life to find it.

Day 6 Matt. 6:24
Can only serve one master.

Day 7 Heb. 10:22-25
Encouraging one another.

Thought for the journey

"I don't know Who — or what — put the question, I don't know when it was put. I don't even remember answering. But at some moment I did answer *Yes* to Someone — or Something — and from that hour I was certain that existence is meaningful and that, therefore, my life, in self-surrender, had a goal."

From *Markings* by Dag Hammarskjold (New York: Alfred A. Knopf, 1964).

Prayer for the journey

Lord, give me the courage to have confidence in your promises and the patience to take one step at a time as I continue my journey of faith. Amen.

Verse for the journey

"When you search for me, you will find me; if you seek me with all your heart" (Jeremiah 29:13).

Appendix

Record information about group members here.

Names	Addresses	Phone Numbers

Group commitments

"Do not be conformed to this world, but be transformed by the renewing of your minds, so that you may discern what is the will of God—what is good and acceptable and perfect" (Romans 12:2).

■ For our time together, we have made the following commitments to each other

■ Goals for our study of this topic are

■ Our group ministry task is

■ My personal action plan is

Prayer requests

Prayers

■ Closing Prayer

Lord God, you have called your servants to ventures of which we cannot see the ending, by paths as yet untrodden, through perils unknown. Give us faith to go out with good courage, not knowing where we go, but only that your hand is leading us and your love supporting us; through Jesus Christ our Lord. Amen.

Lutheran Book of Worship, copyright © 1978, page 153

■ The Lord's Prayer

(If you plan to use the Lord's Prayer, record the version your group uses in the next column.)

Resources

■ Books

Bonhoeffer, Dietrich. *The Cost of Discipleship.* New York: Macmillan, 1963.

Crosby, Michael. *House of Disciples: Church, Economics, and Justice in Matthew.* Maryknoll, N.Y.: Orbis Books, 1988.

Fretheim, Terence E. *Exodus.* Interpretation Series. Louisville: Westminster John Knox, 1991.

Please tell us about your experience with INTERSECTIONS.

4. What I like best about my INTERSECTIONS experience is

5. Three things I want to see the same in future INTERSECTIONS books are

6. Three things I might change in future INTERSECTIONS books are

7. Topics I would like developed for new INTERSECTIONS books are

8. Our group had _____ sessions for the six chapters of this book

9. Other comments I have about INTERSECTIONS are

Thank you for taking the time to fill out and return this questionnaire.

---------------------FOLD CARD IN HERE, SEAL WITH TAPE, AND MAIL TODAY!---------------------

Please check the INTERSECTIONS book you are evaluating.

☐ Following Jesus   ☐ Death and Grief   ☐ Men and Women
☐ The Bible and Life   ☐ Divorce   ☐ Peace
☐ Captive and Free   ☐ Faith   ☐ Praying
☐ Caring and Community   ☐ Jesus: Divine and Human   ☐ Self-Esteem

Please tell us about your small group.

1. Our group had an average attendance of _____.

2. Our group was made up of
Young adults (19-25 years)
_____ Adults (most between 25-45 years)
_____ Adults (most between 45-60 years)
_____ Adults (most between 60-75 years)
_____ Adults (most 75 and over)
_____ Adults (wide mix of ages)
_____ Men (number) and _____ women (number)

3. Our group (answer as many as apply)
_____ came together for the sole purpose of studying this INTERSECTIONS book.
_____ has decided to study another INTERSECTIONS book.
_____ is an ongoing Sunday school group.
_____ met at a time other than Sunday morning.
_____ had only one facilitator for this study.

BUSINESS REPLY MAIL

FIRST-CLASS MAIL   PERMIT NO. 22120   MINNEAPOLIS, MN

POSTAGE WILL BE PAID BY ADDRESSEE

Augsburg Fortress

ATTN INTERSECTIONS TEAM
PO BOX 1209
MINNEAPOLIS MN 55440-8807